BEYOND THE
PROTOTYPE

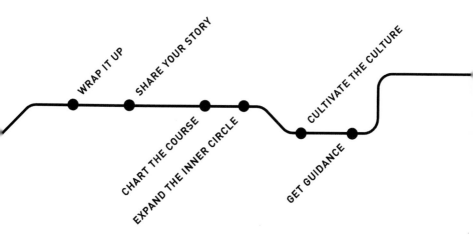

A roadmap for navigating the fuzzy area **between ideas and outcomes**

Douglas Ferguson

Version 1.0

1 2 3 4 5 6 7 8 9 10 KDP 24 23 22 21 20 19

Edited by Emily Brouillet and Kellie McGann
Written by Douglas Ferguson
Designed by Ben Faubion
Illustrations by Mark Peterson & Shawn Bueche

Library of Congress Cataloging-in-Publication Data

Names: Ferguson, Douglas, author.
Title: Beyond the Prototype : A roadmap for navigating the fuzzy area between ideas and outcomes / Douglas Ferguson.
Description: Texas : Voltage Control, 2019.
Subjects: LCSH: Business & Economics --
Library of Congress Control Number: 2019910901
Decision-Making & Problem Solving | Business & Economics -- Entrepreneurship
Classification: LCC
LC record available at https://lccn.loc.gov/2019910901
ISBN: 978-1-7334957-0-7

Voltage Control books are available at special quantity discounts to use as premiums and sales promotions or for use in corporate events and training programs. To inquire, please email sales@voltagecontrol.co

For Tamara, Bowie, Dirty, Sammy, and the Shrink.

CONTENTS

Beyond The Prototype

INTRODUCTION

Introduction

You've got it in your hands. It's just like you imagined. You can't wait to show it off to the world. (Nope, it's not your newborn baby.) It's your prototype.

Before diving in further, don't get scared off or confused by the term "prototype." If you don't think you've ever made one, you probably have. A prototype can mean many things and take many forms. It might be a simple mock-up of the on-demand breakfast taco delivery app you've been dreaming up. Or, your "prototype" might be a vision document that tells the story of the new chain of 4D movie theaters you want to build. It looks like a storyboard of a script, a napkin drawing, a rough draft pitch deck. These are rapid prototypes. A prototype is just a quick simulation of the real thing that you create to uncover deeper insights and expose the riskiest assumptions about your idea.

Maybe you've used your prototype to do some research and user testing that gave you the confidence that your idea has some legs. Maybe it's been tucked away in a drawer somewhere. Whatever it looks like, you have a robust idea, a compelling concept, a set of features, a bundle of consumer insights, or a validated prototype.

But, the burning question is: what next?

That's what this book is all about. It's for people who have struggled to move a critical project forward. It's about those times when you know where you want to go, but you can't get beyond business-as-usual to push it over the finish line. It's about overcoming that slump when you have a notion of what something could be but feel bewildered about how to march forward and build it.

Beyond the Prototype is your guide to navigating that fuzzy area between exploration and implementation.

Sprinting is One Way

As a professional Design Sprint facilitator, I lead companies of all sizes through the five-day Design Sprint methodology, developed by Jake Knapp at Google Ventures. To me, it's one of the best frameworks for jump-starting a project, creating a prototype, and exploring a user-validated approach to any business challenge.

Because of my love for Design Sprints, I've written *Beyond the Prototype* largely from the perspective of this method. Sprints are just one way that people and companies develop ideas. You don't have to run a Design Sprint to get value out of these pages. (Although, I hope you'll be inspired to try one.)

If you haven't participated in a Design Sprint, you'll learn the basics here. If you want to know more, read *Sprint: How to Solve Big Problems and Test New Ideas in Just Five Days* by Jake Knapp, Braden Kowitz, and John Zeratsky.

While I talk about how to avoid common pitfalls post-Sprint, my advice can be applied to any situation when you need to build and maintain momentum around a burgeoning idea. The recommendations here relate to any innovation or design effort where you are struggling to shift from coming up with ideas to making something and putting it out in the world.

Mind the Gap

I've witnessed plenty of companies and teams struggle after their Design Sprint. The path forward isn't as prescriptive or precise. It's a gray area. It's fuzzy. In this gap between ideas and execution, things can grind to a halt or worse, fall apart.

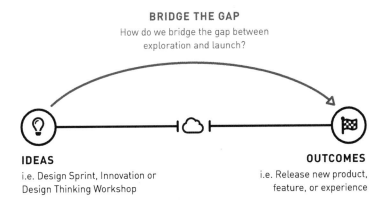

BRIDGE THE GAP
How do we bridge the gap between
exploration and launch?

IDEAS
i.e. Design Sprint, Innovation or
Design Thinking Workshop

OUTCOMES
i.e. Release new product,
feature, or experience

First, your great ideas start to gather dust. Sticky notes fade and fall off the walls like snowflakes. Teams get sucked back into their usual ways of working. More "urgent" initiatives take priority. Momentum wanes. There are many reasons for this: you face tricky internal politics, lack critical design skills, or perhaps you're struggling inside a corporate culture that isn't conducive to launching something like you've envisioned.

"It takes planning and action to move ideas past the early stages of a project or after a Design Sprint. Just as the Design Sprint outlines a clear five-day process, I've created a six-step plan for moving any innovation initiative, vision project, or prototype forward."

You're not alone, though. Even today, most organizations aren't poised to traverse the gap between ideation and execution. Very few move gracefully from discovery-style projects into development and implementation. (Evidenced by the fact that many internal innovation initiatives worry more about number of ideas generated versus outcomes.) The good news is that I've outlined a better way.

Six Steps for Moving Forward

It takes planning and action to move ideas past the early stages of a project or after a Design Sprint. Just as the Design Sprint outlines a clear five-day process, I've created a six-step plan for moving any innovation initiative, vision project, or prototype forward. The tactics emerged from my experiences and learnings with clients including U.S. SOCOM, the Air Force, Adobe, Dropbox, Fidelity, Vrbo, Liberty Mutual, Humana, SAIC, World

Bank, and IDBC. These experiences have helped me uncover the recommendations I'm sharing here.

A Sneak Peek of What's Inside:

+ I delve into Design Sprints and what can happen in the post-Sprint slump.

+ How to reflect on your project, tie up loose ends from the sprint, and craft a story that you can share with others.

+ Insights on how to make a concrete plan for extending your work while growing and supporting the right team.

+ The importance of fostering a culture that can sustain this type of work and guidance on when and how to get expert coaching.

+ Bonus: All of my recommendations for planning and executing a very successful Design Sprint.

Sprinkled throughout *Beyond the Prototype*, you'll also find my favorite nuggets of wisdom from innovation leaders, expert tips, practical activities you can do tomorrow, and stories from top companies.

Pay attention to the six critical moments I spell out, and you'll be able to maintain rigor and keep things moving toward execution. Through this book, I'm your coach and guide to the post-Sprint life. Imagine me alongside you, facilitating, keeping everyone on track, and pushing you toward your ultimate goal.

BEYOND THE PROTOTYPE
Six step plan for moving your
innovation project forward

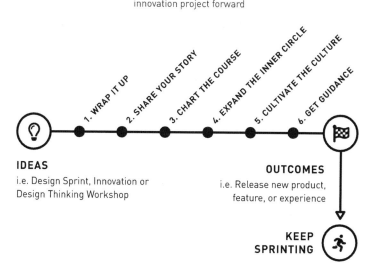

IDEAS
i.e. Design Sprint, Innovation or
Design Thinking Workshop

OUTCOMES
i.e. Release new product,
feature, or experience

**KEEP
SPRINTING**

Legend

Here's what to look for in each chapter

WISE WORDS
Quotes from my interviews with
innovation thought leaders.

SPRINT STORIES
Anecdotes and brief
case studies.

PRO TIP
Little tricks, ideas,
and suggestions.

IN PRACTICE
Strategies and methods you
can use right now.

DESIGN SPRINTS 101

Design Sprints

I wrote *Beyond the Prototype* from my perspective as a Design Sprint facilitator. Design Sprints can be run a lot of different ways, so to make sure we're on the same page I'll provide some background and details on the sprint I'm referring to in this book.

While at Google Ventures, Jake Knapp created a week-long process for tackling unwieldy business problems. He called it, "The Design Sprint." Over five days, the sprint takes a team through a design thinking-based process to uncover insights, prototype an idea, and test it with users.

Why Should You Run a Design Sprint?

+ Align a team around a shared vision.

+ Answer critical business questions.

+ Discover the essence of a creative challenge or problem.

+ Cut through endless internal debate by building a prototype that your customers can give real time feedback on.

When Should You Run a Sprint?

+ When kicking off a new initiative.

+ When looking for new breakthrough features for a product.

+ When you need to switch gears or iterate on a current product.

+ When your team is stuck and needs help deciding a next direction.

+ When you haven't talked to your users enough.

+ When you're misaligned as a team or unsure what direction to take with your product or service.

The Process

The sprint is a tried-and-true formula, with clear plans and activities for each day:

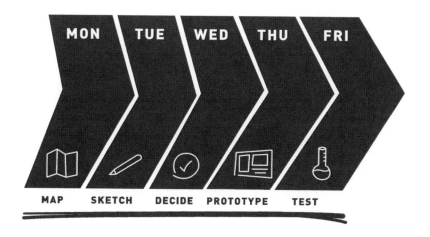

Day 1 | Map: Day one is about making a plan and getting focused. The first day's activities help you define key questions, your goal, hear from internal experts and pick an area of focus.

Day 2 | Sketch: The second day gets everyone's creative juices going. But, instead of group brainstorming, the process prioritizes individual sketching of solutions.

Day 3 | Decide: On day three, the team looks at the potential solutions and works together to decide on what to storyboard and prototype.

Day 4 | Prototype: On day four, the team creates a rapid prototype based on your storyboard, so you have something visual and tangible to test with users.

Day 5 | Test: On the final day, you show your prototype to five different users in one-on-one interviews to gather feedback and get a gut-check on your possible direction.

The Design Sprint Mindset

Through a five-day sprint, you gain first-hand experience not only with specific activities but a completely new way of thinking. It's these mindsets or attitudes that you first learn in the sprint that you'll hear a lot about in this book.

"The insights found through the sprint exercises can be transformative to the way teams work."

Design Sprints are laser-focused on solving one specific problem and helping teams gather information to make a decision. The side effects that come from spending hours with the same group of people while managing big conversations and trying to create change are huge.

The sprint requires that teams work together to break down complex problems while embracing quick-and-dirty prototyping. Sprints also require participants to observe and learn from end-users and communicate in new ways and incorporate feedback faster than they're used to.

The insights found through the sprint exercises can be transformative to the way teams work. As Ambar Muñoz, Senior Product Manager at Adobe shared about their sprint: "The structure of the Design Sprint enabled our team to hone in on the crux of the problem from a user perspective and walk away with an actionable strategy." One week can bring a project to a new level or save months of time and resources. The shifts in mindsets and bonding that teams experience during the short time together is also valuable in changing how teams work. These benefits are salient and undeniable, but there is no guarantee they will last and is at risk of getting lost in the post-Sprint slump.

WISE WORDS

" The big idea of the sprint is to take a small team, clear the schedule for a week, and rapidly progress from problem to tested solution. "

-Jake Knapp,
creator of the Google Ventures Design Sprint

Beyond The Prototype

THE POST-SPRINT SLUMP

WHY TEAMS STRUGGLE AFTER A SPRINT

The Post-Sprint Slump

Design Sprints can be transformative for companies and teams, but unfortunately, they're not magic. They can create alignment through intense focus on an issue, product, feature, or next step. But, to build what you started in your sprint, you'll need more than just five days.

You might be in a post-Sprint slump if:

+ You never reviewed your sprint learnings as a group to make a plan for next steps.

+ You were only able to run a three or four-day Design Sprint and don't feel like you went as deep as you needed.

+ The sprint team went back to status quo and isn't meeting regularly or advancing the project forward.

+ You have no idea how you would take your prototype to the next level of design and testing.

+ You haven't been able to adopt a test-and-learn approach to decision making.

+ You don't think you have the right in-house skills and expertise to keep progressing.

So, before diving into the six steps to combat the slump, what are some of the big reasons that teams or organizations falter after a Design Sprint?

Dropping the Mindset

You can run sprints all day long, but if you don't champion the sprint mindset and act on it, the work's not going to go anywhere. Your Design Sprint created a North Star (or a portion of it) that your team can work towards. The creativity and ideas unleashed in the sprint desperately need discipline, structure, and follow-through if they're going to get anywhere.

You might have colleagues wonder why there is so much to do *after* the sprint. Weren't you supposed to get six months of work in five days? Yes, a Design Sprint super-charges your productivity in a week, but there is still weeks or months of work ahead. However, know that you are much further along than you would have been if you had simply followed your typical ways of working.

While the sprint process opens up big ideas and calls for big shifts in the way work is approached, the hope is that what happens in the five days becomes more than just something a team did one time. Real change begins when the mindset and ways of working permeate everyday routines and tasks.

Teams can struggle if they follow the rules and agenda of a sprint, but don't commit to adopting the principles and ways of working after the sprint. It's easy to get together in a conference room and commit to collaborate, experiment, and prototype more—but what does that look like day-to-day?

WISE
WORDS

❝ The post-Design Sprint slump is real, especially in a small company. While the leadership team understands the power of methodologies such as a Design Sprint to tackle big problems, short-term goals such as urgent customer migrations or landing the next big enterprise deal usually take priority. The key is to keep the conversation alive with minor progress checkpoints, and clearly earmark the larger deliverable in the roadmap. ❞

-Pradeep GanapathyRaj,
VP of Product at Zipwhip

Avoiding Rejection

If the ideas you came up with during the sprint challenge the status quo, you might run into people who oppose the ideas and say they can't be done. Your new ideas and ways of working are at risk of being rejected.

Maybe there are other initiatives that are considered more important, or maybe there are just too many "good" ideas floating around your organization. Or, you may run into funding issues. As Steph Cruchon, CEO of Design Sprint LTD, shared: "I've found it common for the team to run into budgetary issues because there is no project yet. Budgets are tied to projects, the Design Sprint just revealed a new project and thus there is no budget allocated for it."

A lot of organizations have barriers towards new visions, products, or directions—whether explicitly or unintentionally. Most organizations (and people) are highly resistant to change. How much resistance will vary. Do you work at a large, legacy company with entrenched ways of working? Or, are you at a small start-up that perhaps has the opposite problem—no clear processes in place yet? Fear of rejection keeps many teams from taking their sprint plans to the next level. But—it doesn't have to.

Let's Get Going

Ok, I've perhaps worried you a bit with all that can go wrong after a sprint. Whether it's losing focus, forgetting what your True North is, hitting barriers, or fear of rejection, there are concrete ways to overcome and plan for all of them. I'll show you how.

Beyond The Prototype

WRAP IT UP

UNPACK WHAT
YOU LEARNED

WRAP IT UP

Wrap It Up

While a Design Sprint lasts five days, the work doesn't come to a stop at the end of the week. There are still outstanding questions to wrap up your sprint and move to the next phase of work. Most importantly, your team will need to take dedicated time to reflect on what the prototype told you about the hypothesis and questions you had going into user interviews. What did your customers tell you? What did you learn? What's still unclear?

What Did You Learn?

Every team goes into a Design Sprint with assumptions. You most likely believe users like certain ideas or features and design your prototype to test those assumptions. Kai Haley, Head of Design Relations and Lead of Sprint Master Academy at Google, explains more about this idea: "The way we think about Design Sprints at Google is that we develop a hypothesis. And then we test it to get the data to help us decide if that's the direction we're going to take. Ultimately we don't want to launch something that we haven't validated in some way. The decision-making is not the critical moment; it's *'Does this have legs? Do we feel like this is something we could learn a lot from? Is this the general direction?.'"*

Let's use my fictional (but tasty-sounding) on-demand breakfast taco delivery app as an example. You went into your sprint with the desire to test whether customers would want to order breakfast tacos using voice activation and have them delivered by a drone.

You hypothesized the answer was: "heck yes!" You also went into testing with some specific questions you wanted answered: Would people trust a virtual assistant to get their order right? Would they feel comfortable with a drone coming to their home? Would they be worried that their tacos would be cold?

By the end of your sprint, you would have tested these questions, asked users directly how they felt, and have a solid idea of what to do next.

With this concept of assumptions and key questions in mind, your first post-Sprint activity would be gathering as a group to review what you learned and what you didn't learn, what you need to dive into further. This is the wrap-up. A key point to remember here for the team: this isn't about winning or losing or that something did great or poorly. It's about concrete learnings from real people that help you dial-in what you are going to do next.

Reflect as a Group

While you might be tired after five days of sprinting, don't procrastinate on gathering the sprint team to talk about what you've achieved. You'll still have unanswered questions, observations that beg more scrutiny, ambiguous answers, and actionable next steps for the way forward to discuss. I refer to this conversation as a retrospective meeting.

Ideally, start this conversation at the end of your last sprint day. Capture the group's thoughts—it can be as easy as using a whiteboard or stickies. Ask what they thought were their big takeaways from the week. This first meeting can get the conversation going, but avoid going too deep because you want to give the team adequate time to synthesize before you craft a solid plan for what comes next. I recommend you schedule a formal retrospective for the Monday or Tuesday after your sprint. You want to establish that your sprint team, or some part of it, is going to keep building on your Design Sprint work even after the sprint is finished. This conversation will help you uncover the primary ideas you'll want to communicate in your sprint story, which we'll discuss in the next chapter.

Ask the team to come to the meeting with notes and observations of what they experienced and ideas for what to do next. The purpose of this meeting is to agree on the significant learnings that came out of the sprint and potential next steps. Aligning the team like this is vital to moving forward and crafting a narrative everyone can get behind.

WISE WORDS

" It's never about the 'winning' idea. People have that misconception that you're pitting five ideas against each other. Usually, we're looking at a number of different approaches and we're testing a couple of things. It's less about the winning idea and more about 'What are we going to learn here?' That's the point of the sprint: it's a tool to gather the data to make a decision. "

-Kai Haley,
Head of Design Relations and Lead of Sprint Master Academy at Google

SPRINT
STORIES

Testing Hypotheses with Online Art Buyers with TWYLA

Before founding Voltage Control, I was the CTO of Twyla, a start-up that sells limited edition contemporary art prints. Since Twyla was backed by Google Ventures (GV), we had the good fortune of participating in a Design Sprint run by GV. Twyla had launched just a few months before, so the sprint was an opportunity to explore and dial-in our value proposition and shopping experience with people who might be open to buying art online. In that week, the team created two prototypes to explore diverging ideas and approaches in how we talked about the art and explained the product.

We were looking at questions like: Do people want to learn about the artwork through a short, compelling explainer video by the curator? Would people enjoy browsing and buying art through a Tinder-like interface? Would people want to use a try-before-you-buy service?

There were many learnings from that week, but two stand out to me. First, it served as a powerful way to demonstrate to the entire company the efficacy of user testing before launching features. In addition to testing our big ideas, we decided to test a small feature that we had been poised to launch— a price breakdown that showed what the art cost to produce and what the artist would get paid. Everyone assumed that the transparency around pricing and artist fees would be interesting for buyers. But, through just five interviews, we found that users not only didn't like this feature, it deeply annoyed them.

We had put a good amount of time and energy into almost releasing this feature without knowing if our users actually wanted it or if it would encourage them to buy. Another concept we tested was a try-before-you-buy feature for the limited edition prints. Because Twyla art is a luxury product (framed prints are in the thousands of dollars), customers responded to this idea and felt that it would encourage them to order and see the art in their home, but something wasn't quite right. They didn't trust the promise—it seemed too good to be true. So, after the sprint, we iterated on the language in the prototype to be crystal clear about the fact that there were no-strings-attached.

After four iterations of testing we finally had a validated prototype that we were confident we could go build.

Again, we had questions going into the sprint and ideas about what customers would like and not like - some things were true, some weren't, and some needed more tweaking and testing.

When planning a Design Sprint, account for this "long tail" of work that has to be done to act on the learnings (positive or negative) that emerge from the sprint as well as addressing any unanswered questions.

PRO
TIP

If you want to give sprint participants a chance to capture their thoughts before you meet to reflect on the retrospective, think about making a Mural (an online whiteboard) where people can share learnings or send out a quick survey through SurveyMonkey™ or Typeform™. Having this information ahead of time can jumpstart the conversation on the day-of.

37

WISE
WORDS

" **The essential post-Sprint activity is to define which questions have been answered and which are still open—then get to work on tackling the remaining ones.** "

-John Zeratsky,
*former Design Partner at Google Ventures
and co-author of Sprint: How to Solve Big Problems
and Test New Ideas in Just Five Days*

Which One Are You?

One of the things to talk about in your retrospective is how you think the sprint went overall. Sprints can go in all sorts of directions, and all have different potential outcomes. Sometimes sprints go well, sometimes they require us to pivot. How did your sprint go? Talk about how your sprint fits into one of these buckets:

Did you knock it out of the park?

+ This might be you if: your prototype really killed it. Many of your assumptions were right, your users loved it, and you know exactly what to do next.

Was it a learning moment?:

+ This might be you if: You made something interesting during the sprint, but users told you that your idea needs more work. Just like Twyla's try-before-you-buy feature, you'll need to tweak the prototype and do further rounds of testing and explore different approaches until you nail it.

Or, was it a big bummer?:

+ This might be you if: whomp whomp. Just like Twyla's pricing breakdown, the sprint process, prototype, and testing told you that you should go back to the drawing board, take a different tactic, or even abandon the original path.

Every Outcome is a Good Outcome

No matter where you ended, it's all good. That's the point of a sprint—deep and directional insights in five days instead of diving into months of development and then finding out when it's too late to make a change.

Even if the sprint suggested that you need to tweak or pivot, that's a huge win. Imagine instead having spent late nights and countless resources on a project for months only to find out no one wants it, or the design is majorly flawed. When you're open to hearing feedback after just five focused days, you're on the right track.

Every sprint reveals important information. If you're truly trying to create something that people want and need, you'll value this information and care about heading in the right direction.

 **IN PRACTICE**

Capture & See What You Learned

One of our guiding principles at Voltage Control is to always be learning and evolving the sprint practice. A way we do that is through creating custom tools that help us run sprints more effectively. One example is the Voltage Control Design Sprint Scorecard. It's a Google Sheet for capturing in-the-moment learnings, quotes, and answers to your top questions during user interviews. (You can find a link to this resource at https://www.beyondtheprototype.com/resources). More importantly, it's an at-a-glance summary of what you learned through your sprint.

It's useful for staying organized as a team and consolidating notes while conducting user interviews. It's also invaluable after your sprint; it supports less-biased discussions about what you heard from users and how your questions were answered. (i.e. Did they like XYZ feature? No lengthy debate needed—you'll see the answer quickly in the graph generated.)

You started the sprint off with a goal and, through prototyping and testing, you questioned that goal. The scorecard helps you determine how confident you can say whether you hit the target and what questions need more investigation. It's a practical tool that provides a framework for talking about next steps and story themes to share out. (See fig.)

Scorecard Example

Does the user understand the overall concept?

Would the user feel compelled to share with others?

Would users want help from a customer service rep?

Would they use this daily?

Would they want to find out more?

Did the user find the shopping cart?

Did the user watch the video?

Summary:

+ Your Design Sprint doesn't end with a hard-stop on day five. One of the key post-Sprint activities is reflecting on how your hypothesis and questions were answered through testing.

+ Schedule a formal team retrospective for the Monday or Tuesday after your sprint.

+ Come to a consensus on what you learned, what you still have questions on and what might be next.

+ Reflect on how the sprint went overall: was it a big win, a learning moment or a bummer? Whatever it was, the learnings are the important pieces to take moving forward.

SHARE YOUR STORY

SHOW WHAT YOU ACCOMPLISHED

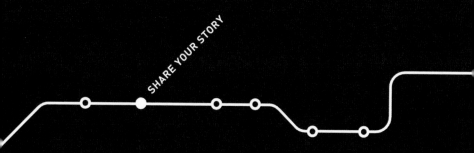

SHARE YOUR STORY

Share Your Story

When your boss asks: "How did the sprint go?" your answer shouldn't be: "We had fun!" While sprints can be enjoyable, your leaders likely want to hear about outcomes. This is the first step in the post-Sprint journey: craft the story of what happened. It's time to share all of the juicy information and learnings from your sprint with those who weren't there.

Over the five days of the sprint, your team went through a journey. There was a starting point (beginning), days of ideating, iterating, prototyping (the middle), and then there was user testing and results (the end). By considering what happened in your sprint as a story with a beginning, middle, and end (although it will surely be more complicated than that) you can begin to formulate and share the narrative of what happened.

Often teams finish sprints excited to make their prototypes a reality and simultaneously a little exhausted from the week of sprinting. It's easy to forget to reflect on what was accomplished. Telling the story of what happened is a huge part of moving forward. The story helps get other people bought in, reminds the team of their own journey, and sets the focus for where they're going next. Ideally, you start crafting the short story of your sprint on the last day of your sprint and continue to evolve it as you go. If your sprint team doesn't tell the story of what happened, someone else will.

Nail the Content

You started gathering learnings and stories from your sprint through your retrospective; now it's time to think about how you are going to share them. Likely, your higher-ups, stakeholders, or fellow employees will be looking for the "meat"—what came out of the time (and perhaps money) invested?

Here are some questions to answer as you shape the story:

+ What triggered the Design Sprint?

+ What's the big headline?

+ What were the top customer insights?

+ Did you receive any adjacent benefits—i.e. increased morale, leadership opportunities, new skills?

+ How do you plan to proceed?

+ How will you measure success?

+ How will you decide to stop pursuing the project?

Another thing to be mindful of as you craft the story: is anything potentially controversial? Are you sharing something unexpected or "out-of-left-field"? Did the sprint capture things that might be uncomfortable for the team to hear? (i.e. "People *really* don't like the direction we're going with our product.")

If so, be sensitive and deliberate about how you share the story and anticipate questions through your narrative.

Shape a Shareable Story

You've gathered your sprint team and done some reflection on what happened, where you ended, and what's next. It's time to put it in on paper (or more likely, online). If you hired a facilitator, they will likely deliver a summary.

All good stories are about problems. Lucky for you, your sprint was based on trying to solve a problem. When you craft the story, start with the beginning. Remember to talk about what the problem looked like at first and how it was affecting your customers or primary users. Data, numbers, and facts are incredibly valuable, but the story you can tell about how something impacted an actual person is what really gets people bought in. Start with describing your initial business challenge, what you wanted to find out from users and why that led you to sprint.

Continue the story of the sprint by sharing the approaches your team took to solve the problem. Get creative, use stories and quotes from team members, share questions, photos of the team, screenshots of the prototype, learnings, failings, and everything in between. No matter how you end up telling the stories, do it with excitement, bring the audience into the moments of the sprint, the good, the bad, and the ugly parts.

Finish the story by using the outcomes we discussed earlier. Whether the end looks like moving forward, tweaking, or pivoting completely, each outcome is positive and necessary. Tell the story of what the future looks like, how your team will proceed, and how the feedback and learnings informed the next steps. The end of the story is the future of the project and is really just the beginning.

Let the Users Speak

One of the superpowers of the Design Sprint is the feedback you get from users. If you recorded user interviews during your sprint, you can easily create a highlight (and lowlight) reel of video testimonials. Include a few of the most relevant clips of your users reacting to your prototype. You not only want to share the positive feedback; it's equally impactful if your users contradicted any assumptions you may have had going into your sprint.

**PRO
TIP**

For more advice on how to broach difficult conversations, I recommend two books:

Nonviolent Communication: A Language of Life by Marshall B. Rosenberg, PhD

Radical Candor: Be a Kick-Ass Boss Without Losing Your Humanity by Kim Scott

WISE
WORDS

"If you're going to do something innovative, it's probably going to be controversial in some way internally."

-Neil Soni,
author of The Startup Gold Mine

**PRO
TIP**

A screencast is a quick and compelling alternative to Keynote™ or PowerPoint™ for telling your story. A screencast is a recording of your computer screen with audio narration. I love that they are easy to make and allow you to share your sprint story widely without a big video production. In your screencast, talk about the goals of the sprint, how the prototype worked, a few big learnings, and what's next.

WISE
WORDS

" In order to win over teams on ideas, the communication piece matters so much... it's the difference between getting stakeholder buy-in and sponsorship or not. "

-Cam Houser,
Founder/Chief Innovation Officer of 3 Day Startup

**PRO
TIP**

Consider the visual design and storytelling aspects of your readout presentation.

Many organizations are accustomed to seeing boring, boiler-plate PowerPoint™ slides. Spend a little extra time (or make friends with a graphic designer and copywriter) to create decks that will make your colleagues and stakeholders want to pay attention. For extra inspiration, read Nancy Duarte's book *Resonate: Present Visual Stories That Transform Audiences.*

54

SPRINT STORIES

Prototypes Speed Up Conversations

I've done a series of Design Sprints with Fidelity, the financial services company. They were preparing to create a product in a highly regulated sphere and also a highly emotional one. Through these sprints they found solutions that allowed them to gracefully navigate this tricky space. After the sprint, they had a concrete, tangible prototype of the product they were going to build.

Fidelity knew that just because they solved these issues for their customers, it didn't mean that they had anticipated all the internal dependencies and regulatory hurdles within their own organization.

The team used their prototype to share the approach, what research had been done, and what this new product really looked like with the broader organization. Historically they had to rely on more ambiguous written documents. Having the concrete prototype provided them a visual and self-explanatory method to socialize the initiative and build consensus with stakeholders. Our client, Suzanne Schmitt, now the VP of Financial Wellness at Prudential, shared: "While at Fidelity, I used the Design Sprint to help drive departmental wide understanding of our product requirements and customer insights. The prototype served as an excellent storytelling tool."

The prototype helped this particular Fidelity team create alignment within a huge organization, something that's much harder to do through words alone.

The tangible prototype helped tell the story and allowed colleagues to quickly surface and address areas of conflict and come to an agreement about what was next.

If the team had pushed forward based on assumptions and without complete alignment in the organization, they would have run into barriers and issues months later. It would have been much more costly. This is the power and benefit of having a story and a prototype that people can see and feel. It changes the trajectory of the project.

SPRINT STORIES

Learnings Inspire Others to Push Harder

A couple of years ago, I ran a Design Sprint for Vrbo, the Austin-based vacation rental company. The sprint brought together a diverse team comprised of different working groups to define an approach for an offering based on emerging travels trends that they believed would be highly competitive in the market. While planning the sprint, I had the opportunity to speak with several of the team members about the opportunity they were exploring. It was clear to me that the team had wildly-divergent opinions on how to position the offering. Unsurprisingly, that resulted in lots of passionate debate throughout the week. Luckily Jake Knapp (author of *Sprint*)] anticipated and accounted for this in the Design Sprint activities.

An expert facilitator and consensus-building methods like "Note and Vote" and "Straw Poll," empowered the team to make decisions and ultimately, build a prototype for testing with users.

A week later, Adam Schwem, Senior Software Engineering Manager, was teeming with excitement as he prepared to share the team's Sprint story at the company's Town Hall. As Adam remembers: "When we presented our sprint story it immediately had a ripple effect through Vrbo. People from areas of the company I had never interacted with approached me asking 'How do I do what you just did?' I'm still regularly asked years later about it; it's really changed the way the whole company thinks."

Stories motivate others to realize that they are capable of more. When we communicate stories in a way where people can see themselves in the narrative, they become empowered to say to themselves, "I can do that too."

 **IN
PRACTICE**

Create an Elevator Pitch

You'll want to create an elevator pitch, or super-short summary, of what you accomplished or learned in your sprint. One activity I recommend to achieve this is "Guardians of Change," which comes from the facilitation group MG Rush. This method helps you decide on the story to tell your key audiences.

Here's how it works

Start by identifying your audience and answering two questions:

1. **What do we tell our bosses or superiors?**

2. **What do we tell people dependent on our results?**

After identifying the target audiences, ask for each, "What are we going to tell _____?" and list the messages as bullet points.

Once agreed upon, MG Rush suggests writing something they call a "3-30 Report."

It's a summary that you write in 30 minutes or less (in other words, don't overthink).

It should take no more than three minutes to read. Bam! You've quickly got something concrete to share with busy execs.

Summary:

+ Remember, if your sprint team doesn't tell the story of what happened, someone else will.

+ Don't procrastinate on crafting your narrative. You can begin by simply talking with the sprint team about what you achieved. Start this conversation at the end of your last sprint day.

+ If you have any unexpected or potentially controversial learnings, think about how you want to approach these conversations with colleagues.

+ Capture the beginning, middle, and end of the story of the sprint and find a way to communicate it with key stakeholders.

+ It's always effective to share cuts of video or audio clips from your user interviews to support your big findings.

CHART THE COURSE

FORMULATE THE
PATH FORWARD

CHART THE COURSE

Chart Your Course

The research, ideas, outcomes, and user interviews that you accomplished through your sprint are great—but unless they're moving you forward, what's the point?

As I mentioned at the beginning, every sprint ends with the question: what's next?

"What's next?" is an overwhelming thought, especially after five intense days of exploring every possible avenue, every question, and trying to figure out the next right step.

In some cases, the sprint showed you and your team that you need to make a major pivot or change—maybe even abandon the beloved idea. In other cases, you'll need to make smaller changes that require more research and user testing (and maybe even run another sprint). And if your sprint got great results, you'll be looking to bring your idea into reality.

No matter where your sprint left you and your team, to take any steps forward—you have to make a plan.

Making a plan forward for a big project can be tricky, and in some cases, it's harder than the sprint itself because it's a much longer journey. It's not just five days you're planning for—you have to get real about your priorities and roadmap for at least the next quarter. To start formulating a path forward, let's start with the end goal you hope to achieve and architect the plan backward.

"With all the different possible avenues to take out of a sprint, it's important to get clear on what you're working towards."

Plot the Route

With all the different possible avenues to take out of a sprint, it's important to get clear on what you're working towards.

Depending on your organization's size, maturity, and goals, the next steps might be high stakes (launching a new product or pivoting to something new) or little experiments like testing new features. It could be something your organization is entirely comfortable with, or maybe it's new for your team, and you're charting new paths for the organization. To navigate this new way forward, it's important to create a clear vision to communicate to everyone involved.

Let's think through a few examples of after-Sprint end goals you might want to achieve:

+ Design and develop new features

+ Overhaul your product architecture

+ Create a new process or service

What exactly did your sprint teach you about your initial idea? Create a one-sentence statement that outlines your new, informed goal.

If during your sprint, your team researched new features for your taco app and discovered users wanted a taco truck review feature most, your next step might be: **We will add a review-a-taco feature under each post to our app.**

If your team came into the sprint with the idea of introducing an octopus taco but found out your audience didn't trust buying octopus from a taco truck, your next step might be: **The team is going to research three new alternatives and find the most viable delicious taco.**

If your team tested a taco tracker service and your customers found it confusing, your next step might be: **We will go back to the drawing board and tweak the language, explainer videos, and images to clarify the message and then re-test with users.**

A lot of the heavy lifting in this section will be supported by the work you did in the "Share Your Story" chapter. If you have a good story, making the plan and getting people on board will be much easier.

Milestone Moments

Once you've decided on your end goal, you can create a plan that helps you get there. Almost always, I recommend that people create plans and measure them in milestones, not in days and weeks. Milestones are moments broken out of the process that create a linear journey for your team to follow. Of course, these milestones allow you to track your progress on your bigger goal, but they also allow you to celebrate the little wins.

They help build confidence and renewed focus to stay committed in a long journey of creating something. It's like when you first decide to learn a language. You can't just say, "I'm going to become fluent in Spanish." That's not how it works. First, you must learn the alphabet and focus on reading a menu at a restaurant. Then the next milestone, and the one after that.

How do we decide which moments are milestones in the process towards bringing an idea into reality? That all depends on where you're going.

WISE
WORDS

" I think if you start well, you finish well, and if you start poorly, you finish poorly. If people really want to be successful in innovation you have to do hard work upfront putting the right foundation in place so that whatever structure you build on top will stand up for a long time rather than come crashing down around your head. "

-Braden Kelley,
author of *Stoking Your Innovation Bonfire*
and *Charting Change*

PRO TIP

Think about the politics of your plan. What are your current business objectives?

What does your organization or leadership want to see next? Quick wins? If so, you should probably focus on tweaking features that you know users desire. Or, is your org aiming for breakthrough innovation? If so, there will be more appetite for longer, more exploratory work after your sprint.

Models for the Path Forward

The most common path forward is the path of: **more research**. This path is for you if, after a sprint, the results are mostly positive, but there are still a lot of questions. The questions you asked in the sprint brought up even more questions and you're left feeling confused with what comes next.

This is the murky area between Design Sprints and development. This can be a tough transition as there isn't a clear blueprint for this in-between zone. Sometimes this phase is called foundational design. It's the phase when your team will expand upon and evolve your prototype; they'll need to build out your experience and think through all of the essential elements and interactions.

This can be a hard place to be. The end result isn't as clear as "build it" and that can be disappointing and frustrating. What's important to remember in this phase is that the clarification, research, and questions are vital to the success of your creation.

Another path forward is the path of: pivoting and re-assessing.

If during your Design Sprint you realized that your ideas need big changes, more than researching smaller elements, you may need to make a big pivot. This might look like revisiting your problem statement or embarking on additional exploration and discovery work to hone in on what you really want to do next. If this is the case, you can run more Design Sprints (or use elements of the sprint) to get closer to the end solution you want to build. Here are a few ways we've found to work well:

Iterative Design Sprints

Take what you learned in the first sprint, synthesize the learnings, and run a new sprint around a revised challenge. Create a fresh prototype based on the most important insights from the last time around.

Parallel or Nested Design Sprints

Looking to produce a wide variety of solutions? Organize simultaneous Design Sprints on the same problem to provide even more divergent ideas. Or, break down your problem and then divide and conquer by having multiple teams of sub-teams running parallel Design Sprints. Either way, coordinate check-ins between the teams for lunches or during a daily readout to ensure transparency and visibility into each other's work.

Cutting Room Floor Iteration

In your first sprint, you probably came up with solid ideas that didn't get prototyped. Based on the feedback you heard during your interviews, identify unanswered questions and high potential sketches that didn't make it into your initial prototype. Explore them in a new prototype and test with additional users.

The last path forward is for those who had a "home run" of a Design Sprint. Things went perfectly, and the idea was expanded upon and ready for development. In this case, the way forward is to create a plan for execution. Write down the moments you're going to measure in the process and gather the team to start executing.

Moments to Measure

To create your plan and milestones, consider the following:

+ What exactly are you trying to accomplish?

+ Who needs to be involved?

+ What research and testing is needed?

+ What needs to happen to make it a reality?

+ What phases in this process are there?

+ What barriers might get in the way?

+ How will we measure success?

+ How will we know when to move on or pivot?

With your answers to these questions and the model path forward that best fits your situation, begin to construct a timeline of milestone moments. Walk yourself and your team through each one and ask, "If we accomplish all of these, will we get our desired result?" Ask team members if there's anything missing and share your plan.

Share the Ugly Baby

Ed Catmull tells the story in *Creativity, Inc* that all Pixar movies start as ugly babies. They describe them as ugly babies to actually make critiquing them easier. They share their movies in early stages with a trusted group called the Braintrust, even when the movies are admittedly half-baked. This allows them to align on direction and course-correct early. (There's even a good story about the one time they didn't do this and almost had a huge mess on their hands.)

In following the advice of Catmull, no matter what your specific project is and how far along, sharing prototypes and ideas with customers should remain vital in the next phase of work. Your newly-created plan is a prototype, make sure to share it out, validate it, tweak it, share it again, over and over as you go. A simple dashboard with status, milestones, and your metrics are typically all you need to get feedback.

Continue to test features, concepts, prototypes, or ideas with users and tweak your designs as you go. Slowly but surely, through prototyping, user testing, design, and technical exploration, you will come to something that you can move into development, so you can get it out into the world for real people to react to.

Measuring Your Success

As you're creating your plan and looking for milestones to use as markers, you'll also need to consider how you will track and measure the success and failure of your effort. Have you ever seen a fundraising thermometer posted to a wall? This simple paper drawing makes a big difference. It's a constant reminder about the project and a visual encouragement to keep pushing further. So many corporate projects get put on hold because of short-term distractions. If you have a constant reminder like meeting cadence or posted metrics, you're more likely to make incremental progress.

Once you discover something you can use for your project, share it often. Consider using metrics like the ones below and mapping them out on your plan.

Sample Metrics

Business Goals:

+ Revenue

+ Acquisition Cost

+ Expenses

Customer-Specific:

+ Product Engagement

+ Retention

+ Referrals

+ Number of Customer Service Calls/Week

Other Metrics:

+ Number of Experiments Run/Month

+ Number of Customers Interviewed/Week

+ Employee Satisfaction

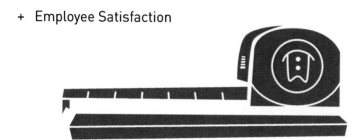

Communication Cadence

You start telling your story after the sprint, and you don't stop as you move into your next phase of work. It's not going to work to your advantage to sweat silently over something for months and then pop up with bad news. Your recommended communication cadence should be part of your plan. Keep your team, organization, boss, and key stakeholders informed at regular intervals. This will help you communicate quick wins and incremental change, which can build internal support and excitement as you work toward your ultimate goal.

Decide when you will deliver reports or readouts to your groups. Get your meetings on the calendar to establish transparency and a project drumbeat. Then, when things go off course, or you run into roadblocks, there will be ways to share, inform, and work with colleagues to move forward.

**WISE
WORDS**

" **There are innovators whose
success is the learning, not
the dollars. Those innovators
will come up with the thing
that works because
eventually there will be that
intersection— the learning
will lead to something that
works in the market, and
then it'll take off.** "

-Navin Kunde,
*Manager of the Open Innovation team
at The Clorox Company*

WISE WORDS

" The people who are responsible for innovation are measured by ROI and not by the number of things that they've tried. I think there should be a structure that rewards people for coming up with ideas, trying them, prototyping them, and being experimental. "

-Julie Schell,
Executive Director of Learning Design, Effectiveness and Innovation at UT Austin's College of Fine Arts

WISE WORDS

" The number one thing I do is try not to tell people about things, but let them use things. You can put something in somebody's hands, and they go from naysayers to feature-requestors so fast. If I can put something in their hands or on their screen where they can click through, it's a much different experience... "

-Jeff Marple,
*Director of Innovation, Corporate Legal,
Liberty Mutual Insurance*

SPRINT STORIES

Liberty Mutual Navigates a Pause After a Sprint

Jeff Marple and Bob Taylor are part of an innovative legal team at Liberty Mutual. They contacted me because they were interested in partnering with another big player in the legal space. If the collaboration had legs, they knew it would mean real revenue potential for both parties. I facilitated a sprint to help them see if the offering and partnership were worth pursuing.

Through the sprint, Liberty Mutual and the partner were able to confirm that they did want to work together, in part because the combination of their data would be incredibly powerful. Much more powerful and insightful than either of them alone. But, how did they shift from sprinting to planning what's next? I sat down with Jeff to talk about how Liberty navigated that fuzzy area after the sprint and made a plan for moving forward.

Jeff told me that the project is still moving forward and that they'll be announcing the partnership in the next year or two, although they did have to navigate a pause after the sprint when the partner was focused on some internal changes.

This pause could have meant a huge loss of momentum, but the Liberty Mutual team was conscious of their partner's situation, didn't push too hard, and stayed patient as they waited for them to be ready to move again.

During this pause, Liberty Mutual instituted two other key strategies to ensure steady progress. First, they named a project manager: "We've found this invaluable," Jeff says. "Having one person assigned to not losing momentum can go a long way. We find this to be incredibly helpful as we move from idea to launch."

"Buy-in is crucial. No plan is good enough to succeed without it."

Then, they created a more robust justification for the collaboration. For that they needed a rock-solid business case. Jeff shared: "We started to pull together information to make a stronger case than we'd already made. We had buy-in to run the sprint, and now we needed buy-in to make the product. It's another level of rigor that has to occur."

Buy-in is crucial. No plan is good enough to succeed without it. Liberty Mutual knew they had buy-in even though their partner was moving slowly. Slowness or non-responsiveness is not always an indicator of lack of desire to proceed. In this case their partner had other priorities at the moment.

When planning your project, consider the whole picture. Do you need to build support and buy-in, do you need to be patient with your allies and be prepared to move when they are ready?

 **IN
PRACTICE**

Leverage User Story Mapping

A Design Sprint is all about learning quickly by getting valuable user feedback on a prototype. But, it does not give you the detailed information you'll need to shift into development. So, as you move from the exploratory phases of your work into design and dev, one of the most invaluable activities is User Story Mapping. User Story Mapping is an alternative to traditional development backlogs and feature-focused development. It's about telling the story of your software or product through a holistic picture of the experience. Jeff Patton describes this technique in his book **User Story Mapping: Discover the Whole Story, Build the Right Product.**

"You know how you mapped your user's journey in your Design Sprint to understand what problems to focus on? You'll need to do the same thing with you your solution - because if you can't imagine it, you can't build it. Map your solution, and break it down into details and options to help you move forward into planning and building a successful product."

-Jeff Patton, author of User Story Mapping

How to make a user story map:

1. Start with a large blank wall or whiteboard. You'll need a good chunk of space for mapping out the user journey.

2. Identify the major user activities across the top or X-axis. Jeff calls this the "Backbone." As you read from left to right, the user's story should unfold through high-level moments or activities. For example, if you were designing a new grocery delivery app, the activities might be: Make List, Search for Items, Add to Cart, Review, Confirm, Engage with Shopper, Delivery, Follow Up.

3. For each activity, list the major tasks that the user does at that moment below. This is your Y-axis. Back to our grocery example: if the Activity was "Engage with Shopper", the user's tasks might be: "approve changes" and "asks for replacements."

4. Continue this process and go as deep as you want by creating subtasks, exceptions, or specific challenges that users face for each task and activity.

5. Use your map to have conversations with stakeholders and developers and create what Jeff calls "release slices"— a subset of tasks that creates a minimal viable release.

User Story Benefits:

+ Ensures the entire team (from PMs and execs to designers and developers) have a shared understanding of what you're building.

+ Keeps your users front-and-center. Avoids out-of-context or myopic focus on individual features.

+ Acts as a framework to plan your MVP, a set of releases, your long-term strategy, or to brainstorm new ways to answer user challenges.

User Story Mapping: The Missing Link

Summary:

+ After you've reflected on the outcomes of your sprint, your next big task is to make a concrete plan for the next phase of work.

+ Depending on your specific organization, you might be making a plan for any number of next steps, from designing and developing new features to additional prototyping or research.

+ Often, organizations find themselves in the space between Design Sprint and development. You may need to bridge this gap by having a team go into more in-depth prototyping and design before development.

+ If you need more exploratory work to get you closer to execution, there are many ways to deconstruct the Design Sprint —from parallel sprints to sprinting on important features from your development backlog.

+ Decide how you are going to track and measure the progress of your effort.

+ Determine your communication cadence for sharing project status reports with your stakeholders and leadership team.

.

EXPAND THE INNER CIRCLE

GATHER THE RIGHT PERSPECTIVES AND SKILLS

EXPAND THE INNER CIRCLE

Expand the Inner Circle

To accomplish anything, you need the right people. The right team can be the difference between months of pushback, frustration, and confusion and a seamless effort towards a shared goal.

In the sprint, your team tested, researched, and prototyped an idea. The initial sprint team had a very specific purpose, and each person on the team was chosen for having unique perspectives and skills. Now you likely need to expand and grow your sprint team to accomplish the next phase of work.

Building the right team is about aligning and complementing the right perspectives and skills. You need the visionary and the executor, the technologist and the empath, the people who have diversity of perspectives and skills.

It's like getting the right team together for a medical procedure. You need the right mix of specialists and nurses to operate, and an admin to schedule everything. You wouldn't want to assemble a team with a dentist instead of a heart doctor or mix up information on exactly what was needed to be done. These small nuances and details in the team can make a world of difference in what gets accomplished.

In an ideal world, your sprint team is the execution team, but the post-Sprint team isn't always the same exact group. This decision is largely informed by the outcomes and plan you've already established from your sprint. Sometimes you'll discover insights that change your understanding of who you need on the team. If your sprint went incredibly well and you're onto the development stage, you might need more developers on the team. Your sprint team will likely still be involved, just expanded and shifted, but shouldn't be a completely new team.

When you have the post-Sprint plan of attack, you have the blueprint for building your team. Different plans and projects lead to different kinds of teams.

While there's no exact formula for who or how many people to put on your team, there are some systems and structures to be aware of when assembling everyone.

Governance Structure

Who is responsible for what? From the very beginning of time, humans have organized themselves into groups with self-governing structures. We need to know who is in charge, who is leading, and who will follow. This sort of organization has helped us exist in roles that use our unique talents and function together efficiently. In the same way, when you're executing a sprint plan, it's critical to create this same sort of structure.

In the times I've seen teams skip over this step, things have gotten off track quickly. While ownership and accountability might seem obvious at first, eventually, if these things aren't written down, you'll find that decisions don't get made or you might run into power struggles between people or groups.

When you create this governing structure, it can illuminate who exactly is needed on the team, who might be missing, and who will be in charge of making it all happen. You can lean on the structure to provide support to anticipate and move through the trickiest of times.

The easiest way to put this all down on paper and avoid miscommunicating is to create a chart of responsibility. Use whatever works best for you and your team, but my recommended tool is the RACI matrix. It's a chart that maps out every task, milestone, and key decision that goes into finishing the project and assigning responsibility. (See the In Practice section at the end of this chapter for more detail on making a RACI.)

It can be confusing and frustrating to be a part of a team and be unsure where you belong or what your exact responsibilities are. When the opportunity to succeed isn't clear for teams and individuals, it's hard to be bought into the success. By creating a chart like this and making sure everyone understands and agrees with it, a unity that is often overlooked is fostered.

Each member of the team can clearly see who they report to and who they are responsible for consulting along the way. This can change the communication dynamic and make sure everyone is included and heard throughout the process.

**PRO
TIP**

A RACI matrix is only one option for planning governance and responsibilities. If it doesn't work for you, explore other models.

For example, Atlassian uses something they call DACI for efficient decision-making, which stands for **Driver-Approver-Contributors-Informed.**

89

**PRO
TIP**

A team charter is another tool you might want to put in place at the beginning of your project to ensure clarity and focus. A team charter outlines things like: your team's purpose, project scope, time commitment, deliverables, reporting plan, and desired outcomes.

WISE WORDS

It's not so important to have the right degree, to have the right set of experiences. It's more important to have the right mindset and to have the willingness to go and do stuff that is uncomfortable or may seem like it might be beneath your station. We really tried to find people who have the courage and the lack of ego required to get things done in that way. It's more about the people than it is about the process.

-Taylor Dawson,
Founding member, GE's FirstBuild

A Well-Balanced Team

There's no scale to measure exactly how well-balanced a team is. It's not just getting a mix of the right people with the right skills; it means finding people with the right (and unique) perspectives as well.

Have you ever been on a team with too many cooks in the kitchen? Everyone pulls in a different direction and no singular decision-maker has the power to steer. This unbalance leans too heavy on leaders and not enough doers.

The same can happen with visionaries and executers. Some people are great at thinking big picture, blue sky ideas, but too many of those people and your idea will stay in the clouds forever.

Gather a mix of team members who are open and optimistic and a few who are realistic about what your organization can do. As much as you can, strive for a group with diversity of all kinds—including gender, sexuality, and race, as well as seniority and experience level. If you're wondering who these people are in your organization, here are some other characteristics to look for:

Multi-functional: Multi-functional team members are extremely valuable assets to any post-Sprint team. These are people who can wear many hats and contribute in different ways. The design consultancy IDEO has referred to people like this as "T-Shaped." IDEO CEO Tim Brown describes it like this: "The vertical stroke of the 'T' is a depth of skill that allows them to contribute to the creative process. That can be from any number of different fields: an industrial designer, an architect, a social scientist, a business specialist or a mechanical engineer. The horizontal stroke of the 'T' is the disposition for collaboration across disciplines."

A few examples of a T-shaped person: Someone who can write a kick-ass presentation *and* create wireframes. Or, someone who can facilitate empathetic user research *and* do visual design. Or, a teammate who can project manage *and* can help you navigate the politics of your company.

Entrepreneurial: When you are doing something new, you have to be comfortable with uncertainty. Look for colleagues who can navigate ambiguous challenges and situations. Identify people who are excited to chart new territory and do something that hasn't been done before.

Collaborative: Members of a team like this also need to be ready to work closely with others. The post-Sprint lifestyle isn't for those who want to be heads-down doing their own thing. Look for a team of people who are comfortable bouncing ideas off of others and giving (and receiving) feedback.

Flexible: As your team builds the new product, feature, or experience you prototyped in your sprint, there will be ups and downs. Staff your team with people who are ready for roadblocks and changes in course and the not-so-exciting moments.

SPRINT STORIES

Too Many Designers

I recently had the opportunity to run a sprint for a prominent software company working on a mobile design of their design product. All signs pointed to a good outcome: the client had a new Product Manager, the team had a ton of experience, and their leadership had charged them with really moving the needle on a new mobile strategy. So, I was a bit surprised when the sprint didn't run as smoothly as I had hoped.

We started the sprint on day one with mapping our idea and problem we were trying to solve. There were significant questions about who the audience was and what they needed. What kept happening though, was that the sprint team kept discussing and focusing on the exact words they were going to use in marketing. They spent hours talking about the names of landing pages, forms, and ads all mixed together.

Looking around the room, I pinpointed the issue—there were too many designers on the sprint team.

While the product was a design product and we were able to produce compelling assets for our prototype, we found that we had significant gaps in our knowledge of the problem at hand. This was because the company had over-indexed on a single perspective for the sprint team—in this case, design and marketing. When you don't have enough diversity of thought and perspective in your sprint, the power of the week is almost guaranteed to be squandered.

The results of the sprint absolutely would have shifted with a different mix of participants. We did the best with what we had and were able to pivot that first day and make sure the non-designer voices in the room were heard.

Even if you're designing a product for designers, you still need more than designers on the team. Don't forget to keep your post-Sprint teams balanced regardless of what you're building.

WISE
WORDS

" Figure out who are the champions and who understands long-term thinking. It's probably the space that kills innovation in large corporations time and time again. Having a long-term mindset is incredibly difficult for publicly traded, large corporations these days. That is not what most companies either have the luxury of thinking like or the tolerance for. "

-Katherine Gilbert Manuel,
Operating Partner, IDEA Fund Partners

"If you're looking for your team to create something new and exciting, it can be more effective to put them in a new or different environment."

Make Space

Don't have the project team sitting in your typical business setting if they are working on out-of-the-box thinking. If you're looking for your team to create something new and exciting, it can be more effective to put them in a new or different environment.

Inevitably, sitting at their same desk, the daily grind of work will get in the way and take priority. Their coworkers will always know how to find them if they need a favor or want to talk about the movie they saw last night. These things aren't inherently bad, but they're opportunities that can take away from the creative sprint mindset.

Some teams come together from different departments and even work in separate buildings or drab cubicles, this is never ideal for teams working on an innovative project. Even if your post-Sprint team has work to get done in addition to the sprint work, you'll want to encourage creative, collaborative work between everyone daily.

How you design your workspace can shape how well you will work together. Here are a few thoughts on creating a space that fosters connection and increases productivity:

+ **Sit Together**: If the team is working on the project together, try moving desks, so the team is physically close together and can communicate quickly and easily.

+ **Huddle Space:** Create a project space or "war room" for the team where you can hold meetings, pin-up work in progress, and share work with others.

+ **Buy Sticky Notes:** These are the markers of start-up culture for a reason. Ensure that your team has tools for design and collaboration at their disposable—i.e. whiteboards, sticky notes, and Sharpies™.

**PRO
TIP**

If you have team members working in different cities or locations, consider how you will set them up for successful, pain-free collaboration.

Have all of the necessary tools in place such as a good video conferencing tool, project management tools like Trello, and a Slack channel for communication. Also, if the budget allows, plan for regular sessions when the team works together in the same location.

SPRINT STORIES

Better than a Trust Fall

The work that teams are doing during a sprint is often deep, transformative work. Not only in the initial five days but in the weeks and months after these teams and their newly added teammates must commit to finish the journey of creating something new together.

Naturally, it binds teams together without cheesy team building activities that are normally found when trying to force teams to "bond."

In a sprint with Dropbox last year, I saw a beautiful example of this. They were a brand new team, and most of the participants had never worked together before. They were eager to learn more about each other. It was even one person's first day on the job, who was anxious about starting the job in such a unique way. While they were exploring the problem space in the beginning of the sprint, they were also learning about each other and establishing rapport, trust, and all the elements needed for collaboration.

Through the sprint, they gathered deep insights into where their users struggle and how to better position support and community tools.

Additionally, the team bonding and connection-making that the Dropbox team experienced through the sprint may have been even more beneficial to the company in the long term. Should you run a sprint with the secret goal of getting people to work better together? Maybe.

 **IN PRACTICE**

How to Create a RACI Chart

Designers and creatives are often allergic to formal business tools—Excel spreadsheets and Gantt charts send shivers down their spines. However, when shifting to the more-executional phases of a project, I always recommend making a RACI chart.

A RACI is a simple matrix that outlines the roles and responsibilities of a complex project. Having a RACI in place ensures that all stakeholders and team members know their part, who is doing what, and who is the ultimate decision-maker.

R	R	I	I
A	C	R	R

Step 1: Know the Roles

Before you assign your stakeholders a RACI letter, know what each role means:

R **Responsible** A team member who is doing the work directly.	**A** **Accountable** This is usually the ultimate decider. The person who is going to review work and/or decides what gets the green light.
C **Consulted** Those individuals who should be brought in to review and give feedback on work, often based on their particular expertise.	**I** **Informed** People who are kept up-to-date on the project at critical milestones, but aren't in the daily grind of every decision.

Step 2: Identify project roles or team members

Determine the important roles (i.e. UX designer, content strategist, marketing director, developer, subject matter expert) that will be working on this specific project. List these across the top row of your matrix. (see figure)

Step 3: Identify key tasks and milestones

Think through the main milestones, deliverables, or activities for your project. (i.e. Create a research plan, facilitate user interviews, lead synthesis, create the final document.) List those down the left side of your matrix.

Step 4: Assign a letter for each person

For each person involved, assign a letter that matches how a specific task relates to them. Voila!

RACI in Action

Deliverables	PM	Designer	Strategist	Copywriter
Protype Output	R	R	I	I
Confirm Copy	A	C	R	R
Gather Photos	A	C	R	I
Create Ads	A	C	I	R

Need Facilitator Skills?

A final consideration: are you going to continue to hold Design Sprints or other types of testing and ideation? If so, you will need a person on your team (or available as required) who can facilitate sprints, creative working sessions, or user testing. If you don't have someone on your team or within your organization who can do this, you may need to bring in an outside coach or facilitator.

There is a ton of material out there on participatory design techniques, but being good at facilitating is a professional discipline. It takes practice and time to perfect and master. Having someone with experience and expertise will bring better results if your plan has you continuing sprints or other workshop techniques.

Summary

+ Your sprint team will probably need to grow based on the needs you identified in your project plan.

+ Create a RACI matrix to determine governance structure and responsibilities from the very beginning.

+ Build a diverse team that has the right mix of leadership, entrepreneurship, skills, and vision.

+ Ensure that your team is poised to work collaboratively. If possible, have the team sit together and create a war room for meetings and regular pin-ups.

+ Consider bringing in a design thinking facilitator if you are going to need additional sprints.

CULTIVATE THE CULTURE

INSPIRE THE SPRINT MINDSET

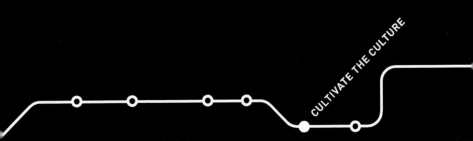

CULTIVATE THE CULTURE

Cultivate The Culture

At this point, you've prepared and planned how to approach your post-Sprint life and assembled a team to help you take your idea to the next step.

With this groundwork in place, the project is moving but what happens when your team hits a bump, starts to slow down, and approaches the slump again?

In 2017 I ran a Design Sprint for the Austin-based delivery start-up Favor. Their goal was clearly defined from the start. They wanted to increase the hourly earnings for their runners while decreasing runner frustration. The team put themselves in the shoes of the runners and asked hard questions about how to improve their work.

In the days of the sprint, they innovated, researched, and prototyped new concepts to solve their problem. Team members lit up while they shared new ideas and other teammates responded in open ways to hold positive discussions. Some would sketch the idea concept on the wall and before I knew it there were dozens of innovative ideas on sticky notes around the room.

This is what it looks like when a sprint goes well. A difference I often see in sprints that go well and sprints that lag is in the adoption of the sprint culture.

While sprints are made up of steps and research, it's the culture and mindset that's behind the process that can really transform a team and even an entire organization.

The Favor team knew they wanted to work more in the sprint style, but they hadn't gotten there yet in their day-to-day work. Once they had one sprint under their belt and had seen how the process of working quickly, collaborating, and focusing on a clear goal could transform their results, they knew they wanted more. It didn't take long before their organization adopted the principles of a sprint into their daily routines.

P.J. Tanzillo, their Head of Product, said about the experience, "It reminded our team how valuable prototyping and early user feedback can be in building great designs."

The Favor team not only had a successful sprint but had tremendous follow-through on their sprint ideas and innovations. When their team came up against barriers, they used the culture from their sprint to quickly innovate around them. With this new way of working in place, their corporate culture completely changed. This is a power of the sprint that's not often highlighted.

By fostering a culture in your team and broader organization that is supportive of innovative work, the ideas that took root during the sprint can have fertile ground to grow and thrive in. And you might just transform an entire working culture.

"The underlying principles that you adopted for your five-day sprint are often the inspiration and impetus for new ways of working."

Developing a Sprint Culture

The maxim "know thyself" is relevant here. Is your company poised to promote innovative, entrepreneurial culture? And, even if they say they are ready, do they really mean it? If the answer is no to either question, you'll need to actively work to establish the internal habits that align with this kind of work. The underlying principles that you adopted for your five-day sprint are often the inspiration and impetus for new ways of working and approaching problems after the sprint.

Some attitudes and approaches I find most important are:

+ **Speedy, but Focused**: Your team should be ready to move fast in the right direction. On the other hand, don't move so fast that you forget to properly frame your problem and make a plan with clear milestones. Don't chase speed for speed's sake. Teams that make this mistake fail to disrupt anything—they're just disruptive.

+ **Experimental:** Everything the team explores on the project won't be for keeps. Wireframes will be made and thrown out. Features will be tested and abandoned. Encourage and give the team the freedom to experiment with different things.

+ **Bite-Sized:** To reduce the "blast radius" of your project and the potential for leadership freak-out moments, break the work into small, manageable pieces.

+ **Curious**: Typically, companies try to validate assumptions they already have. In sprint culture, you need to look at learnings with curiosity. Be open to findings from your users that contradict what you thought.

+ **Long-Term Thinking:** Most companies are used to measuring projects based on ROI (Return on Investment). Yet, the projects that grow out of Design Sprints are often more about long-term gains, not short-term profit. I like to focus less on return on investment and more on "learnings" from investments.

🦉 WISE WORDS

❝ It is very difficult to have an innovative organization if the leader is not absolutely committed to it because it's a leadership issue. It's not a minor process change, a suggestions scheme, and one or two razzmatazz brainstorm meetings. What you need is a serious commitment. You need to change people's objectives, and you need to change the mission, the communication, and really get behind it. You need to empower people to try things.❞

-Paul Sloane,
*Keynote Conference Speaker & Expert Facilitator
on Innovation & Lateral Thinking*

WISE WORDS

" Innovation teams place tremendous emphasis on developing empathy for the users we're designing for, which is so important. But sometimes we neglect to do the same with one another. Empathy within our teams creates the connection and trust that make real innovation possible. "

-Jay Melone,
Partner & Product Strategist, New Haircut

**PRO
TIP**

Vulnerability is another attitude to cultivate in your corporate culture.

Through vulnerability, you can build trust and a sense of psychological safety in your team to know that it's ok to ask for help and to fail. It's key that this vulnerability starts at the leadership level so people can see the behavior modelled at the highest level of the organization. To explore more about the importance of vulnerability, I recommend the books **An Everyone Culture** by Robert Kegan and Lisa Lahey, and **Daring Greatly** by Brené Brown.

114

WISE WORDS

"Any successful innovation program should be structured around a cause rather than a thing."

-Heather Bryant,
Director of Innovation and Impact, Momentous Institute

Everyone's Favorite "F" Word

Successful sprints are made up of many small failures. Failures are the guiding forces in sprints: they show us which directions to avoid, save us months of work on projects users don't want, and help us keep open minds in our work.

In the world of innovation, the concept of embracing failure is a big theme. While failures used to be regarded as largely negative, now they're admired as "learning moments." While talk of failure is looked upon more positively now, it doesn't mean that it's not still scary for many of us. In fact, preventing errors and missteps from ever happening is baked into how most organizations operate and what they measure themselves on. Unfortunately, avoiding errors is not optimal for inspiring innovation. It will stifle it.

Do you remember when you were first learning your times tables in school? The idea of multiplying numbers was brand new and so first, we learned the basics and were told to practice. We did this with essentially every new thing we learned: spelling, geography, science. We quizzed ourselves, practiced with flashcards, and "failed" along the way. Everything wasn't always for keeps. But we grow up, and suddenly we have to get it right from the outset.

"During and after sprints, our focus is never to get it right, it is always to learn first and continually build on that."

The stakes are higher in our jobs and so failure is less of an option. There's no space for "practice." During and after sprints, our focus is never to get it right, it is always to learn first and continually build on that. This change in mindset invites a desperately-needed freedom in the workplace. When I interviewed Doreen Lorenzo, Assistant Dean in the School of Design and Creative Technology at the University of Texas, she said: "Throw out the word failure. In my world, I say I never use the 'F-word.' We need to teach everyone to always be in a continuous learning mode."

So as you are adopting this new culture inspired through sprinting, could you too throw out the "F-word"? Think of this new way of working as an experiment, with the point always being to find out something quickly and improve from there.

**PRO
TIP**

One way to make sure you build a culture that leans into failure (aka "learning") is to communicate your stumbles, as well as your successes.

Start a weekly email newsletter that you send out to your key stakeholders (or whoever else wants to be kept in the loop), and it will be a perfect spot to regularly share what's working, what hasn't, and what you've gleaned from all of it.

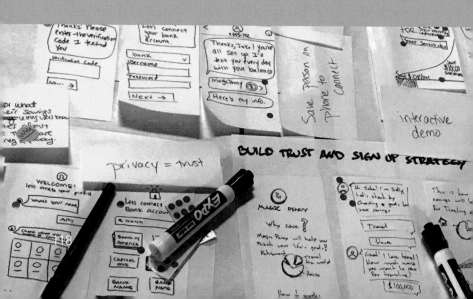

WISE WORDS

" **Our goal has been to grow Design Sprints, but the bigger goal is to mature our design and innovation practice. Design Sprints are a way to have bigger conversations around how we work, how we deliver, and how we design.**"

-Pascal Lola,
  UX Design Lead at Humana

Build In Recovery Time

In exercise and fitness, talk of recovery time is normal—no one blinks an eye. Athletes put their bodies through incredible amounts of training to perform, so of course, they need time to recover after such intense periods of work. In our corporate work world today, the idea of recovery is essentially non-existent. Sure, most companies have vacation policies where you can take a day or two off at your own risk but rarely do we think about recovery time in innovation.

In light of our current obsession with "hustle," we're always asking how quickly we can get the next thing done. I've worked with teams and individuals who have been pushed in that direction and the end results aren't good. Pushing from sprint to sprint and project to project can leave team members experiencing burnout and in some cases, will quit their jobs. Humans aren't robots and need time to breathe.

Innovation work is intense when you're doing iterative user testing, prototyping, development sprints, and the like. If you're well-organized, your team will be crushing it week after week, busting out work and pushing toward critical milestones. By taking the time for your team to have breathers mid-project they're more likely to enjoy the work (and their lives) and produce better work throughout the process. Like athletes, they can't go hard every day. Create time for mental recovery and take a group field trip to a museum or movie.

More than just letting teams take a break, what you're really doing in these moments is instilling and creating a culture that people want to be a part of. In the sprint, you learn to work and push hard for five days. After the sprint, there's not always a clear end date to look forward to; creating breaks helps continue the culture and pace of pushing hard.

Success Gets Attention

Success is contagious. When teams are running sprints well and following through on big changes in their post-Sprint life, more and more teams will want some of that special sauce. In organizations without design thinking or innovation groups, this new way of working will become a curious topic of conversation.

For a culture to catch fire and change an organization, it has to be replicable. Sharing the sprint culture doesn't always have to be done by CEOs and big leaders. It can be done by teams sharing with other teams how their success in the sprint has changed their work.

Here are a few ways you can share your sprint culture with others:

+ Have a presentation ready that tells the story of your sprint and what you learned.

+ Lend out teammates to teach other groups the sprint techniques.

+ Offer to facilitate sprints for others.

+ Invite other team members to observe your team for a day of sprint-like working.

**PRO
TIP**

When you're ready to explore the power of downtime, my favorite book on the subject is **Rest: Why You Get More Done When You Work Less** by Alex Soojung-Kim Pang.

Then, download the podcast **Time Off** from John Fitch, a product designer and entrepreneur who believes that unplugging is "both a skill and a competitive advantage."

WISE
WORDS

‟ **Demonstration of innovative thinking should be rewarded just like delivering on your day job. The way you motivate people is by rewarding them in their career path that the more they swim outside of their swim lane, the more senior they can become because they are demonstrating that they're working on behalf of the firm and not just doing a job.** ”

-Jim Colson,
Independent Advisor, IBM
Fellow—Emeritus and former VP/CTO
of Watson Customer Engagement

SPRINT STORIES

The Home Depot Jumpstarts Sprint Culture

The Home Depot first started using Design Sprints in 2017 to explore a new direction for their home page and then to create new products, solve complex problems, and improve their customer experience. Members of The Home Depot Online Team quickly saw the value of the process and the culture that came out of running these sprints.

As they became comfortable running sprints, they started to scale the methodologies and concepts to transform the way their organization worked completely. Eugene du Plessis, Senior UX Designer, says, "Tackling smaller problems nimbly is what gave us the experience and then the confidence to scale. With that, you gain confidence and experience. You gain understanding, not just knowledge. Gaining understanding is what helps you take it to the next level."

Instead of telling the The Home Depot employees to use Design Thinking in their work, they're actually showing them through facilitated Design Sprints. Brooke Creef, UX Manager, says: "We're teaching Design Thinking by way of Design Sprints. We made a conscious decision to streamline our focus on this methodology instead of a Design Thinking Playbook."

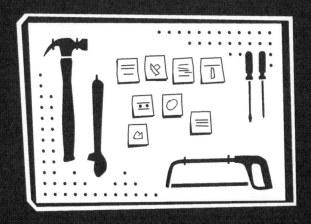

And, it's working—they've built considerable momentum internally. One of the secrets to their success is that they align their sprints to The Home Depot's strategic initiatives. They call this "Inline Innovation." Brooke notes that this connection between the sprint methods and the company's larger goals was instrumental in driving success in the program's first two years.

They haven't tried to force their company to adapt to the sprint, they've actually altered the sprint to fit The Home Depot culture.They did this by designing a Sprint schedule that works for them. "We've adapted the traditional five-day sprint to work more efficiently inside The Home Depot's culture," Eugene said. "Getting everybody in a room for five days is close to impossible. Our sweet spot is three days, including validation." Not only did they adopt the sprint culture, but they didn't abandon their own. By combining the two, they successfully scaled and got the best of both worlds.

With their compressed sprint schedule, focused problem areas, and by training up a team of facilitators, The Home Depot is using Design Sprints as a tool for building an authentic and sustainable design thinking practice inside an organization.

**IN
PRACTICE**

Run Meetings Differently

Sometimes when we champion a new culture at work, we get stuck talking about it and not necessarily doing it. It's like gardening. You can't force a seed to grow into something lush and colorful. You have to set up the right conditions (good soil, water, light) for what you want to sprout.

Instead of sending an email telling everyone about the new "sprint culture," try instead to encourage your team to approach work from the more visual, more collaborative style they experienced in the sprint. Two of the most transformative parts of a sprint to foster with your team are:

1. the collaborative, democratic spirit
2. the emphasis on prototyping

IN PRACTICE

" If a picture is worth a thousand words, a prototype is worth a thousand meetings "

-Tom & David Kelley,
Brothers and partners at IDEO

Here are ways to bring those concepts into your everyday workday:

1. No Prototype No Meeting

At the design consultancy IDEO, they have something called "Boyle's Law," which is the aphorism that you should "Never attend a meeting without a prototype." Named for Dennis Boyle, an IDEO engineer with over 50 patents, the company put this saying into practice by insisting that something tangible is shared at every meeting. This does not mean a physical prototype of the next smartphone you've designed in your off-hours. In this sense, a prototype can be a draft of a presentation, a rough wireframe, or a set of sketches that describes the user flow. Start gathering around the more tangible, and you'll find less talk and more action.

2. Note and Vote

Bringing a prototype to every meeting might not be doable, so an alternative is to get in the habit of holding a "Note and Vote" at more meetings. As Jake Knapp put it so perfectly in a blog post about this technique: "Meetings want to suck. Two of their favorite suckiness tactics are group brainstorming and group negotiation."

Note and Vote is what it says. Use it the next time you need to generate new ideas or make a decision as a group.

+ Begin by "noting"- give everyone quiet time, maybe 10 min, to come up with ideas individually on a piece of paper. In the end, give people some time to edit their list down and cross off the truly insane or embarrassing ideas.

+ Next, everyone should share their ideas, but without doing a lengthy sales pitch. Just state your thoughts and move onto the next person.

+ Lastly, have everyone privately vote on their favorite ideas.

+ End by sharing your votes and seeing what rose to the top.

Note and Vote cuts through the noise and debate, and gets to an agreed-upon decision.

Summary

+ Culture can make or break your post-Design Sprint success. Be sure to support the right environment for innovation.

+ Understand where your organization is and if they are ready to embrace the sprint culture every day. An openness to experimentation, moving fast but deliberately, and curiosity is essential.

+ Failure will be part of your post-Sprint life. You'll design and test things that won't work. Consider ways to continually communicate your learnings to keep people abreast of successes and failures.

+ Don't forget to give your team moments for decompression and breaks from the intense work they are doing.

+ The success of your Design Sprint may lead to interest from other organizations or business units. Be prepared to consult or assist other teams that are sprint-curious. Find easy ways to help spread the culture you're inspiring and "infect" different parts of your company with the goodness!

Beyond The Prototype

GET GUIDANCE

KNOW WHEN TO REACH OUT TO THE EXPERTS

GET GUIDANCE

Get Guidance

Very rarely do things go according to plan. This entire book is based on the idea that it's hard to always stay on track and execute on an idea (especially when so many people are involved).

It's hard to know what to do when we run into problems. Sometimes it's even hard to know what to do when things are going well. What's the right way forward? Where do we go next?

The best way to figure out where to go next is to ask someone who's been there. For many of us, asking for help is hard. We don't want to bother someone or ask a dumb question or seem like we don't know what we're doing. That fear and uncertainty can keep us from experiencing massive and accelerated change by asking an expert for help.

Finding a coach or mentor can save you time, resources, and be your guide through the post-Sprint world.

What is a Coach?

Bill Gates once opened a TED Talk by saying, "Everyone needs a coach." (Interestingly, he uses a coach to help him with the card game Bridge.) He went on to say: "We all need people who will give us feedback. That's how we improve."

A coach isn't a therapist or consultant. In work, they're someone who can help you develop personal or professional traits, strengths, and characteristics. The best coaches don't necessarily even have the answers, but they are great at asking all the right questions.

Maybe you are a new manager of a large creative team and want to know how to better work with designers. Or, maybe you're a product manager for a project that involves many business units and you need help getting silos to collaborate and work harmoniously. Sometimes you just need someone to coach you on being a more patient boss or how to give constructive feedback. Whatever your goals, a coach is someone who can give you actionable assignments or concrete objectives for growing in your role and career.

"Since an outside coach or consultant is a budget item some can't afford, it's smart to start by looking for assistance within your organization."

Go Inside

Since an outside coach or consultant is a budget item some can't afford, it's smart to start by looking for assistance within your organization. Seek out someone who can be your sounding board; someone ready to answer questions on the process of making a new product, to give you an unbiased option on a direction you're pursuing, or to answer a frantic call or email when the crap hits the fan.

Look for an internal coach or mentor who has some of these qualities:

+ **Not too close to your project:** You don't want anyone overly-invested in the outcomes of the specific workstream you're leading.

+ **Savvy in navigating your organization:** A person who knows how to gracefully traverse corporate politics will help you through the sticky points.

+ **Skilled in design thinking, design, user experience, or innovation:** People with this background typically can look at things with a user-centered, critical eye and can provide excellent feedback and direction.

**PRO
TIP**

If you don't have someone inside your company to tap as a coach, another option is to find a mentor from another organization.

Do some LinkedIn sleuthing to find a friend or a friend-of-a-friend with the right background and who might be up for an occasional coffee or phone call.

137

 **WISE WORDS**

" Developing coaching relationships with my clients is about long-term accountability, not just innovation events. There are some simple ways to do it, like a phone call to talk about 'rose, thorn, and bud.' What's something good that's happening? What are some challenges? What's on the road ahead? "

-Daniel Stillman,
Master Facilitator and Conversation Designer

SPRINT STORIES

Coaching a Sprint

Sunroom is an Austin-based start-up that helps renters find homes and apartments and book tours on-demand. The founders, Ben Doherty and Zac Maurais, initially approached me because they wanted help recruiting a software developer to build a website. They had interviewed apartment renters and property managers. These interviews exposed some unmet needs and potential business opportunities so they were excited to start building software to offer these potential solutions. While this approach is better than just assuming the market will want everything you're building and spend a lot of money to create the final product, I convinced them to take another route.

Instead, I encouraged them to hold a Design Sprint or at least create a prototype before building any software. Software takes time and is expensive and after investing time and money, it's often hard to embrace changes even when the customer is screaming that your solution isn't working.

Imagine building a giant office complex without a blueprint or a model, realizing that the parking lot isn't big enough half way through and have to shift the foundation. A prototype allows you to simulate a functioning product or process so that users can interact with it and you can observe their reactions. From there you can make changes and tweak your prototype until you are ready to build. At this point, it is much cheaper to build, because you know exactly what you need and there is no time spent reworking.

After coaching them on these concepts they were intrigued and they bought a copy of the book *Sprint* for the entire team. The next week, they showed up at Austin Design Sprint, my monthly meetup. We talked at length and they were starting to formulate a plan to hold a Design Sprint the following week (they move fast!).

As a scrappy start-up, they found a friend who had classroom facilitation experience and asked if I would be willing to coach her and them through the process of holding their own sprint. We had calls leading up to the sprint to make sure they were prepared for everything from food to supplies and I worked one on one with Dana, their facilitator, to make sure she had what she needed for the week including a facilitator guide and checklists.

During the sprint, all four of us talked each morning and evening to plan, talk about their concerns, and discuss how they might tweak the next day's approach. On the first day of the sprint the team ran into issues on aligning on their goal. I coached them to go back and revisit a few things and they were able to pause and fix it. At the end of the week, they had a prototype.

Since the sprint, Zac says that they've adopted many of the methods and folded them into their work: "We've made them even more lightweight, and something that we can do with a really small team, like two or three people, instead of seven."

Coaching their team through the process may have been even more valuable than facilitating a sprint for them. By showing them how to do it for themselves, they became completely equipped to run and adopt these ideas on their own. (And they always know they have support from a coach if they need it.)

 **IN PRACTICE**

Questions for a Potential Coach

If you want a coach to help you grow as a leader who builds innovative products or experiences, I've pulled together a checklist of questions to ask potential coaches. Tap your personal network to find one to three coaches to interview. Ask all or some of these questions. After, reflect on your chemistry with coach (this is probably most important) and how well their answers line up with your desires and expectations. Make a list of pros and cons for each coach so that you can objectively compare, but don't be afraid to go with your gut. Selecting a coach is often about finding someone you feel comfortable talking with.

Ask the Coach:

☐ How did you get into coaching? What credentials do you have? What is your specific area of expertise, or are you a generalist?

☐ Were you ever a practitioner?

☐ What's your style of coaching? Do you have a specific approach, framework, or process that you use with every client?

☐ How and when do we engage? (i.e. over phone, video, or in-person)

☐ Can you share a success story? Can you share a cautionary tale? (i.e a client you had to fire?)

☐ How will we set goals, outcomes, and measure the results of our engagement?

☐ Do you have your own coach? What's beneficial to you about it?

☐ How do you stay up-to-date on your industry, expertise or coaching methodologies?

☐ Can I "try out" a coaching sessions before committing to a long-term engagement?

Summary

+ A coach is someone who can ask you tough questions and provide you concrete, actionable guidance in achieving your personal and professional goals.

+ If you are not experienced in leading innovation work, consider regular check-ins with a coach who can help you navigate tricky moments and provide general counsel.

+ The first place to look is within your organization. See if there is a neutral party, experienced in innovation or design thinking, who is willing to meet with you to bounce ideas off of and to help you navigate the organization.

+ If you can't find someone outside, look for an outside consultant or coach. The investment can be in-depth or light, and many coaches are open to designing an engagement plan that supports you and the time and money you can commit.

BONUS CHAPTER

EXPERT TIPS FOR PLANNING SUPERB SPRINTS

Plan The Sprint

This book was written to help you wade through the challenges of a post-Sprint life and turn your prototype into a reality. The principles and steps in this book have been tested and tried with hundreds of teams over the years. While I am sure these can transform your post-Sprint life, there is one big thing that needs to go right first: the Design Sprint.

The success after a sprint is determined by how well you prepare for the sprint itself. Things can start to go off course from as early as the initial stages of planning, but if you can start on the right foot, it's going to be easier to continue after the sprint. Without going into all the gory details of planning, let's talk about what I consider the essential elements of success both before and during the sprint.

Before The Sprint

While a sprint takes place over just five days, the weeks leading up to the sprint are critical. There's a considerable amount of legwork needed to make the event itself go smoothly. As you embark on sprint planning, keep these factors in mind:

Ready for Research: Design Sprints are big on incorporating user research and testing a prototype. Talking with your potential or current users will get you quick, meaningful feedback and direction on what you're building. If user research is not in your wheelhouse or expertse, here's the shortlist of things to remember:

Finding People: Start by identifying the qualities you are looking for (i.e. age, income, interests, attitude) and then plan for how you'll recruit. On the casual side, you can rope in friends or family or post on Craigslist or Facebook for people. If you have money to invest, there's also places like Respondent and Ethn.io that can help you find and schedule users to interview.

The Interviewer: Just as you need to identify your facilitator, determine who will lead your user interviews. If you have a professional facilitator, they may do this. If not, UX designers or researchers are typically skilled in this area or may want to build up this competency.

Prep Time: Make sure the interviewer has identified a quiet space where the interviews will take place. They should also prepare a discussion guide for the interviews and be familiar with the Five-Act Interview, which is a structure for a productive user interview.

PRO
TIP

Feel free to play with the roles you include in your sprint depending on your organization.

For example, while some teams have a "Decider" in each sprint, Google specifically doesn't identify one in their sprints. It doesn't mesh with their flat organization. Do what feels right for your team and leadership structure.

Bonus Chapter

PRO TIP

To learn more practical tips about how to run user interviews, read the book **Talking to Humans: Success Starts with Understanding Your Customers** by Giff Constable.

**PRO
TIP**

One of the Design Sprint roles that I have found to be super important is The Stitcher.

For my team, The Stitcher acts like the "Scrum Master" for the prototype, tracking and bringing all the disparate design pieces together. We've even created a custom Mural board to help The Stitcher be more effective. (You can find a link to this resource at https://www.beyondtheprototype.com/resources)

WISE WORDS

" Facilitative leadership is perhaps one of the most important skills in the next 50 years...What are those skills? They're not skills of style; they're skills of substance. It's not knowing the answer, it's knowing the question. It's a skill of being a good listener, not a good persuasive charismatic speaker. "

-Terrence Metz,
Managing Director of MG RUSH Facilitation Training and Coaching

Facilitators are Your Friends

Naturally, I'm biased because I facilitate Design Sprints, but choosing the right facilitator for your sprint is vital. An excellent facilitator is a mix between a party planner (they deal with logistics and scheduling), a sherpa (they guide the group through each activity), and a counselor (they have to know how to handle tough conversations). They may sound like a unicorn, but you can find one!

Out or In?

Your Design Sprint facilitator doesn't have to be someone hired from the outside. They can come from within your organization. Find out if you have a design thinking or innovation group that might be able to help. Or, tap a teammate with the right mix of people and organizational skills.

Unbiased

Your facilitator needs to remain impartial and unbiased throughout the process. They shouldn't have high stakes in the project. The facilitator's distance from the task at hand will let them focus on guiding the group versus trying to steer the conversation in a certain way.

Emotional Intelligence

They need genuine curiosity about people and intrinsic interest in solving problems. Your facilitator should bring a unique blend of flexibility, people skills, and critical thinking so they can deftly manage the personalities in the room.

**PRO
TIP**

If you can spring for it, I highly recommend getting your team out of the office for your sprint.

Check out websites like Peerspace, Liquidspace, and Breather for unique spots to rent. Look for creative, inspiring spots that will shake up business-as-usual attitudes.

WISE WORDS

" We've realized that the strength of a facilitator is directly proportional to the success of the sprint. You can't have low-level facilitators and expect the same results. "

-Eugene Du Plessis,
Senior UX Designer, Home Depot

Plan, Plan, Plan

Once you have your facilitator identified, they will likely spearhead the scheduling, planning, and logistics for the week. There are many details that go into five days of sprinting. Here are the components I always keep top-of-mind:

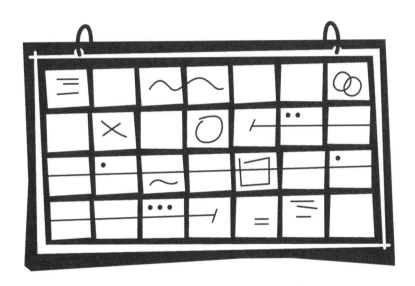

Good Timing: Make sure your organization is ready to run a Design Sprint. Some indicators that it might be the wrong time are: you can't get clear on your goals or you don't have proper buy-in from leadership or the team to think differently both during and after the sprint.

Who's There: Take the time to really think about the participants for your sprint. Not everyone can (or should) be there. Build an attendee list with the right mix of skills, temperaments, and expertise. For example, you'll need one or two people with design chops for prototyping. You need someone who has deep knowledge of your customer, the brand voice, and the market. And, you'll need to determine if you have one "Decider" —that person who will make the final call on decisions during the sprint—or if decisions will be made democratically.

"Pay attention to the little things and you'll reap the benefits of a smoother sprint."

Details Matter: In the book *Sprint*, the authors get wonderfully specific about the supplies needed for the activities. These details might seem small and unimportant (Q: Do I really need these exact markers? A: Yes.), but they are there for a reason. In addition to materials, the different voting mechanisms are important to prioritize and focus on. Pay attention to the little things and you'll reap the benefits of a smoother sprint.

Don't Rush It: Don't underestimate how long it takes to get a Design Sprint going. Ideally, you have at least two weeks to plan so you have everything buttoned up on the Monday of the sprint.

**PRO
TIP**

It might seem like snack micromanagement, but don't overlook the importance of having healthy food on-hand for the team. Donut breakfasts and pizza lunches will inevitably lead to sugar crashes and post-lunch naps. Stock the sprint room with things like nuts, fruit, protein bars and water to get people through the long days.

WISE WORDS

" I advise people to accurately reflect the hierarchy and decision-making model their company follows. If it's a small startup that's driven by one decision maker then the process you use should give the appropriate weight to their role. At Google, we have a flat organization structure so we use a simple democratic dot voting method to select what to prototype. "

-Kai Haley,
Head of Design Relations and Lead of Sprint Master Academy at Google

SPRINT STORIES

Daily Readouts Increase Inclusion

I recently facilitated a Design Sprint for Zipwhip. It was an especially exciting sprint because Zipwhip had just crossed the 300 employee mark after closing their series D. I've found this to be really telling time for a start-up. They have to shed some of their early methods of working and find tools and processes that scale to large groups.

Early on, start-ups have the luxury of inviting everyone to every meeting. As they grow, this inclusive and collaborative culture must be protected and can be a logistical struggle with how to include everyone. Zipwhip's Design Sprint was a great example of this. Pradeep GanapathyRaj, Zipwhip's VP of Product, and the rest of the team had a hard time down-selecting the group, but we eventually got there.

In the spirit of inclusion, we decided to hold a readout each day after the sprint team concluded its work so that we could share out progress and answer any questions that other employees might have.

These daily readouts allowed us to include a wider audience than just the sprint participants and it felt nice to see everyone appreciate that we took the time to loop them in.

Not only did the readout keep important people in the loop, but the questions that they asked us each day inspired us, made us look at things differently, and gave us additional inputs that we took into our next sprint day.

Pradeep also thought it would be helpful to host an Ask Me Anything session during lunch on Wednesday. This was an opportunity for product managers, directors, technical product managers, engineering managers, and scrum masters to learn about the process. The product team was keen to explore how Design Sprints might be folded into the ongoing product lifecycle.

The purpose of this inclusion and communication is to give folks that couldn't be involved an inside look at how the week was progressing; this way, they would understand why decisions were made and the tradeoffs involved. They become your advocates. When the right people are in the loop, they'll feel part of the process and you'll avoid organizational "torpedoes" after the fact.

IN PRACTICE

The Pre-Sprint Questionnaire

To prepare for your sprint, answer the following questions. Share your answers with your team so they know what to expect. Have a kick-off meeting the week prior so that you can answer any questions and set expectations.
(You can find a link to this resource at https://www.beyondtheprototype.com/resources)

General:

☐ Why are you doing this sprint? (i.e. Boost conversion? Reach new customers? Solve a customer problem?)

☐ What existing research or data will fuel the sprint?

☐ How will you measure success?

☐ When do you plan to implement the results of this sprint?

People:

☐ Who is your Decider? (This is the true decision-maker—the "CEO" of this project or even the actual CEO.)

☐ Who is your Facilitator?

☐ Who is on your Sprint Team? (7 people or less! Cover most key roles and aspects of the business.)

☐ Can your Sprint Team clear their schedules for the Sprint? (They need to!)

☐ Who will lead user interviews? (They can be part of the core team or an extra helper.)

☐ Who are your Experts? (You'll interview 2-4 experts, from the core team or outside, on day one.)

Space & Logistics:

☐ Where will you host your sprint?

☐ Where will you conduct the user interviews?

☐ Who is going to order supplies, snacks, and lunch?

Bonus Points:

☐ Are you conducting a daily readout to additional team members?

☐ If so who is invited?

☐ When is your kick-off?

☐ When is your retrospective? (Ideally, it's the week following.)

Summary:

+ User research takes careful planning. Identify who will conduct the interviews and make sure they are comfortable with the interview process and discussion guide.

+ Consider hiring a professional Design Sprint or design thinking facilitator to run your session.

+ Planning is essential before a sprint. Consider where you are going to hold your sprint, sweat all the details, nail down your participant list, and give yourself at least two weeks to plan.

+ During your sprint, consider scheduling a daily readout for stakeholders, don't underestimate the importance of energy-giving snacks, and make sure the group stays on track.

+ And, of course, for optimal results, follow the six post-Sprint steps outlined in this book.

FINAL THOUGHTS

Final Thoughts

Design Sprints are potent.

The magic unfolds in just five days. The time restraint is what makes them especially powerful.

But, after the Design Sprint, indecisiveness, and lack of focus can haunt teams and lead to loss of momentum. Life after a Design Sprint can be daunting— the path is not as prescriptive. It's too easy to slip back into regular patterns. That speed from the Design Sprint is forgotten, decisions don't get made, and time slips through your fingers. Weeks turn into months with little-to-no progress.

Of course, there are endless ways to move beyond the prototype, and this book encourages you first to acknowledge the potential of what you can achieve if you continue to harness the energy created in your Design Sprint.

Start with the critical principles for success post-Sprint as outlined in this book, and internalize them. While the tools and stories can be directly applied, I hope you go beyond mere application. Develop a mindset that prompts you to bring sprint-inspired thinking into every aspect of your work. If you do this, you will build wins-upon-wins as well as wins-upon-losses, nimbly navigating the sometimes-treacherous and always-complex world in which we all find ourselves.

Whatever you do: don't let the momentum of your Design Sprint fade. It takes tenacity and grit. Keep the fire going and make great things.

I'm always interested in learning and growing. As you experiment with the approaches here, please feel free to share your thoughts, positive or negative, with me at beyondtheprototype@voltagecontrol.co. Perhaps, I'll include your story in the next edition.

I wish you the best of luck in your endeavors to bring new and novel things into the world. May your innovations inspire the ones who follow.

Acknowledgments

Many thanks to all of my friends and colleagues who have been there for me and Voltage Control and who read early drafts and gave helpful feedback including:

Adam Schwem

Alicia Griffin

Amr Khalifeh

Ann Ferguson

Anna Jackson

Barry O'Reilly

Ben Faubion

Ben Himes

Bettina Warburg

Bjorn Billhardt

Bob Gower

Bob Taylor

Braden Kowitz

Brett A. Hurt

Brian Sharples

Brian Sisco

Chris Gillan

Christie Nicholson

Clayton Aynesworth

Daina Burnes

Dan Levy

Dan Weingrod

Daniel Stillman

Daniel Walsh

Danikka Dillon

Danny Kim

David Hawks

Deborah West

Eileen Buesing

Elijah Wood

Emily Brouillet

Eric Abrahamson

Erin Mays

Etienne de Bruin

Gary Hoover

Gary Tedder

H.O. Maycotte

Heath Grant

Henrik Johansson

Hillary Leone

Jack Humphrey

Jae Hoon Lim

Jake Knapp

James Mann

Jamie LaFrenier

Jay Melone

Jeff Gothelf

Jeff Marples

Jeff Patton

Jessica Tranchina

Jim Colson

Jim Scott

John Fitch

John Izturiz

John Turpin
John Zeratsky
Josh Baer
Josh Kerr
Josh Seiden
Justin Halloran
Justin Kurynny
Kai Haley
Kalyn Rozanski
Karen Holst
Kegan Blumenthal
Keith Lewis
Keith McCandless
Kellie McGann
Lance Ellisor
Leslie Ferguson
Lilly Davis
Lindsay Lark
Mandy Pitre
Mariano Suarez-Battan
Mark Peterson
Matt Borden
Matt McDonnell
Matthew Robinson
Meetesh Karia
Michael Margolis
Mike Caskey
Morgan Linton
Neha Saigal
Nick Nadeau
Nick Speaks
Noah Kagan
P.J. Tanzillo

Pascal Lola
Paul May
Peter Bell
Peter Nicholson
Philip Jordan
Pixie Renna
Pradeep GanapathyRaj
Q Beck
Quay Morris
Randall Squires
Reagan Pugh
Richard Banfield
Ron Berry
Ross Buhrdorf
Sara Garonzik
Sean Duffy
Shawn Bueche
Sonya Emery
Stephanie Wright
Stephen Straus
Steve Marsh
Steve Meier
Suzanne Schmitt
Tamara Engle
Terrence Metz
Thorsten Borek
Tom Serres
Virginia Ingram
Xander Pollock
Zachary Maurais

About The Author

Douglas Ferguson is an entrepreneur and human-centered technologist with over 20 years of experience. He is president of Voltage Control, an Austin-based workshop agency that specializes in Design Sprints and innovation workshops.

Voltage Control helps companies solve tough problems using integrated decision-making methods. Their workshops are rooted in a philosophy that nobody is as smart as everybody. Layering a diverse set of methodologies including Lean, Agile, Design Sprints, Thinking Wrong, and Liberating Structures, Voltage Control guides companies through complex operating environments and equips them with the tools and structures critical for innovation transformation. Voltage Control has worked with a range of organizations including Capital Factory, US Air Force, Thomson Reuters, Fidelity Investments, Vrbo, and Dropbox.

Prior to Voltage Control, Douglas held CTO positions at numerous Austin start-ups where he led product and engineering teams using Agile, Lean, and human-centered design principles. Douglas is active in the Austin start-up community where he serves on the board of several non-profits, mentors start-ups, and advises early-stage ventures.

Notes

Notes

Notes

Notes

Notes

Notes

Notes

Notes

Notes

Made in the USA
San Bernardino, CA
13 November 2019

59885768R00102